THE SEVEN SWORDS

THE SEVEN SWORDS

By *GERALD VANN* O.P.

With Eight Reproductions
from the Paintings of

EL GRECO

SHEED AND WARD
1953

MANUFACTURED IN THE UNITED STATES
OF AMERICA

ι, 2073

CONTENTS

		page
INTRODUCTION—*The Sinner Who Looks Like a Saint*		3
I	*THE FIRST SWORD*	15
II	*THE SECOND SWORD*	25
III	*THE THIRD SWORD*	35
IV	*THE FOURTH SWORD*	45
V	*THE FIFTH SWORD*	55
VI	*THE SIXTH SWORD*	67
VII	*THE SEVENTH SWORD*	77

ILLUSTRATIONS

From paintings by El Greco

THE HOLY FAMILY   *frontispiece*
Cleveland Museum of Art, Ohio

THE ANNUNCIATION (DETAIL)   *facing page* 18
Museo Biblioteca Balaguer, Villanueva y Geltru

THE FLIGHT INTO EGYPT   28
Baron R. von Hirsch, Basle

MATER DOLOROSA   36
Mrs. Thomas Harris, London

CHRIST TAKING LEAVE OF HIS MOTHER   46
Pelishor Castle, Sinaia, Roumania

THE BURIAL OF COUNT ORGAZ (DETAIL)   58
San Tome, Toledo

PIETA   70
Comtesse de la Béraudière, Paris

MADONNA ON A THRONE OF CLOUDS   80
Luis Rey, Barcelona

PREFACE

THE pages which follow represent the substance of a Lenten series of addresses given at the church of Our Lady of Pity, London, S.W., in 1949. To these has been prefixed an introductory chapter, *The Sinner Who Looks Like a Saint,* which first appeared in *The Commonweal (U.S.A.)* of May 19, 1950; to whose Editor I wish to express my thanks for his permission to use it here. To the Editor of the *Catholic Herald* also my thanks are due for permission to incorporate into ch. V some material from an article which appeared in that paper.

G. V.

Laxton, 9 July 1950

INTRODUCTION

The Sinner Who Looks Like A Saint

AT THE beginning of *The Heart of the Matter* Mr. Graham Greene quotes some words of Péguy: *"Le pécheur est au coeur même de la chrétienté:* The sinner stands at the very heart of Christendom. No one is more competent than he to say what it all means—no one unless it be the saint." The words might indeed form a text for a great many contemporary Catholic novels: you think not only of Greene but of Waugh, of Mauriac. And as you follow the unfolding drama of the lives created by them you sometimes find that in the end the sinner comes to look suspiciously like a saint himself. Are the novelists justified? Can the sinner be a saint?

We shall perhaps find an answer if, to begin with, we examine Péguy's words more closely. Why is the sinner the central figure? Why is he more competent than others to say what Christianity is about? Because Christianity is the religion of redemption, of rescue, of

3

mercy, of God's tenderness and pity; because Christianity means the coming of light from darkness, of life from death: the dry bones live again. And it is the sorrowing sinner who knows this process, knows it in his heart, far more than the ninety-nine who need not penance; it is the sinner who knows the need of a Saviour by more than hearsay; it is the sinner who knows the grace of God not as an empty term in a textbook or a sermon, but as a reality longed for, fled from, gained and lost again, known as a blinded man knows colour.

Clearly we are using the word sinner, when we speak thus, in a special sense. Mary who was a sinner in the city, Peter who denied, out of cowardice, the Christ he loved, all the millions of human beings who fail from weakness to keep the law of God: yes, you can call them sinners, but they are sinners in a very different sense from those who deliberately turn their love into hate, who coldly deride God and his law, who blandly ignore the reality they have once known. These others sin, but they struggle; they disobey God, but they love God or they long to love God; and so it is that in fact their love can become a deep and consuming fire in them, in a way that is unimaginable to the externally pious Christians to whom these buffetings are quite unknown and who perhaps are complacent about their success in keeping the law. . . .

So we begin to understand more clearly why Christ was the friend of sinners; we begin to see a deeper truth in St. Thomas's dictum that the sins of the flesh are less grave than the sins of the mind, than pride and hatred and despair. Fr. Vincent McNabb once said: "When our Lord looks on a sinner he isn't a sinner: he used to be." But does that mean that his sinful habits fall from

4

him like a garment, that he is suddenly and completely free? It may, for indeed there are plenty of examples of the sudden conversion which does bring about a sudden and complete change of character; but it may not, it may mean a different sort of change: a change from being a sinner in the deeper and more real sense of one who hates God to being a sinner in this other more technical and superficial sense of one who loves God but is not yet wholly free. "The flesh lusteth against the spirit and the spirit against the flesh. . . . The good which I will, I do not; but the evil which I will not, that I do." The more one studies human behaviour the more one realises the degree to which it is determined. We have free will, we can choose, we can make up our own minds, yes, but not always, and certainly quite often not completely: there are conditions of mind and body in which freedom is in fact impossible, as in obsessional states; but quite apart from that, there are all the situations in which freedom is not wholly destroyed but diminished, there are all the "enemies of the voluntary" of which we read in the moral theologians; and among these is the *habitus retractatus*—the habit which has been repented of but is not yet eradicated. The sin that goes on; but it is sin *à contre-coeur*, it represents not the deepest but only a superficial direction of the will; and that means more than that the guilt involved is considerably diminished. We must not think too exclusively in terms of warring impulses: the hoped-for issue of the struggle is not just light in place of darkness but light out of darkness: the light will be the greater for the preceding darkness because it is in darkness that the light is engendered; the love will be the greater for the preceding betrayals, because, as with Peter, it is in the sorrow for the betrayals that the greatest love is born. Sorrow is creative.

The sinner then, in this sense of the word, is indeed at the heart of Christendom because it is in him preeminently that the Christian mystery is achieved, the divine alchemy is achieved; the sinner knows better than others what Christianity is about because to him sin and grace, mercy, forgiveness, are not words learnt in a catechism but realities known in the immediacy of bitter experience; and the sinner, finally, may indeed come to look very like a saint because this process that is going on in him all the time, this constant struggling towards the light and constant recession into the darkness, is a process in which love, though he may not believe it, is always increasing and increasing until in the end it may lead him to martyrdom.

Are we then to sin in order that all this may come about in us? Obviously no; not only because in any case the end cannot justify the means; not only because in any case sin is a violence against the nature of God and of truth which no good result to ourselves could begin to justify; but because we should then not be sinners in this sense at all: we should be throwing ourselves into sin instead of struggling against it. And that very fact may correct us if we allow ourselves to think that perhaps then after all our sins do not matter much, or even to pride ourselves on them. It can never be true to say, *Pecca fortiter*: Sin away as hard as you can and then you'll become a saint. If we do we are in fact moving in precisely the opposite direction: we are not hungering and thirsting after justice even while failing to achieve it, we are turning our backs on it. If we deliberately and coldly choose evil, or if we begin to take a

6

lenient view of our sins and to tell ourselves that they do not matter, we are necessarily turning farther and farther away from God, not struggling towards him. And that hardening of the mind to evil has a sequel very far removed from sanctity; for it can end logically only in a frozenness of the will in evil which ultimately becomes immovable, and the soul is then in hell.

What we can and must say is that, provided the struggle is really going on, provided the longing for God is really increasing, then however many the failures continue to be, even though to seventy times seven times, still there is hope because the light and the life are at work beneath the surface, and they will shine forth in *novissimo die*, there will be the music and the feasting for the prodigal's return in the end.

If all this is true it provides us in passing with an answer which is not always adverted to in dealing with the question: If all that is said of divine grace is true, how is it that Catholics are so often no better than their neighbours? There are two answers which are often given to the question: first, that it is easy to see the sins and miss the virtues, which is true; and secondly, that grace is not magic and, no matter what its power to transfigure a personality will not do so and cannot do so unless the grace is used and used to the full: a purely external and formalist frequenting of the sacraments will never make us saints; and that also is true. But there is this third thing: that we tend necessarily to judge by externals—for only God knows the secrets of men's hearts—and therefore to confuse the two senses of the word sinner: the whole of this deep creative process may completely escape us. Two people may act externally in the same way, be guilty externally of the same

7

sin: but in one the process of petrifaction may be going forward, and in the other the power of love may be growing to such proportions that in the end it will turn all to gold.

It is unwise to try to judge men in terms of character alone—a mistake that has been made by more than one moral philosopher. Character is the sum of many habits: it is a part of that training of the will which in turn is part of the aim of education. But only a part. It is possible to have a good character, which means to act habitually in ways which are morally good, and yet at the same time to fail to be a complete human being, to fail in spiritual vitality, to lack something which is revealed by its very absence to be essential, a pearl of great price. The ethic of duty for duty's sake is dead and depressing for just this reason: you are taking right action out of the sphere of vital action because away from joy and pleasure and love. The sort of morality which in fact is no more than a thin-lipped human respectability is but a degradation of the same sort of thing. And there are the same elements, there is the same poison, in any moral life which is no more than a self-conscious and self-reliant striving after the right for its own sake or for the sake of some reward, some complacency, some *réclame*, which it brings. A character may indeed, if you dig down deep enough, reveal itself to be no more than a *persona*, a façade built to impress either the world or its own maker. That is why it is of little avail to train the will to choose the right and resist the wrong unless at the same time you are training the whole personality to see and to love. The pursuit of the right can be as sterile as remorse; what is creative and life-giving is the vision and therefore

8

the love of truth and goodness and beauty. Augustine said, not "Too late have I found the clue to right action," but "Too late have I loved Thee, O Beauty ever old and ever new."

In other words, we shall never understand Christianity so long as we see it exclusively in terms not of poetry but of prose. There are indeed numberless lives which could be called prosaic in no pejorative sense: simple lives which follow an even course, free of struggles and crises and tensions, and which, always faithful, always devoted, end by achieving great sanctity, though it is probably the sort of sanctity which remains unsung. These are already at an infinite distance from the pure character-builders: for it is God, and therefore love, they serve, and a life which looks externally very humdrum may in fact be very precious precisely because it is so simple in the philosophical sense also, so unsullied, so single-minded, so sterling, so pure. But there are the poetic lives also; and perhaps they too are legion. There are the "wrestlers with Christ" we have been thinking of: the lives whose poetry is dramatic and perhaps epic. There are the men and women—and perhaps still more the children—whose poetry is lyrical: their whole lives a constant outpouring of love expressing itself in ways which seem sometimes to defy the categories of a reasoned philosophy, for indeed it is not reason but the holy Spirit that moves them and makes them so unpredictable to more earth-bound minds. *Organum pulsatum a Spiritu Sancto:* to be the perfect instrument for God's fingers, producing divine music; to be so completely one with God, so completely filled with his life, that you can say I live now not I, but Christ liveth in me: that is the consummation of the Christian life, and it is

9

there that character becomes wholly transfigured into holiness, the virtues wholly taken up into that higher life we call the Gifts of the Holy Ghost, the prose wholly transmuted into poetry. And because this is the consummation, it is to this that all the different kinds of Christian life come in the end: not only the lyrical children of God, not only the wrestlers who come to him through much agony of spirit and the morass of sin, but the ones also who at the first were so prosaic, the good and faithful servants who have been faithful in little things, they too enter, in the end, into the joy of their Lord.

It remains true that it is the sinner who is at the very heart of Christendom: there is one further question we must consider. If it is true that the sinner, more than the externally pious Christian, can know the true meaning of Christianity; and if on the other hand it is true that the Christian may not for that reason sin, what is he to do?

For most of us the question is very quickly answered. We tend to think of sinners in terms of people whose sins have had some dramatic quality about them, a notoriety perhaps, or a physical or mental disintegration: but why should we? The constant sins of the tongue, the petty vanities and cruelties, the narrow-mindedness and lack of vision, the vacillations of faith and hope, the small dishonesties, the sloth and self-centredness of many a respectable life: these are sins enough in all conscience; these are material enough for any exploration of the depths if only we will not blind ourselves to their true character. What we need is not more sin but more sense of sin.

But there are, thank God, the others, the golden-

10

hearted ones who are always very close to God's will: what of them? Perhaps we need say no more than that one of the Gifts is called Understanding: it enables the soul to penetrate the inner meaning of ultimate realities —and if of love, of redemption, then certainly of the sin which the love redeems. There is no love without sympathy; but sympathy means experiencing directly in oneself what another is suffering. You could not be a saint without a sense of sin; and indeed it is one of the most strikingly obvious things about the saints that their awareness of sin is such that they sorrow over their to us imperceptible peccadilloes far more than we over our gravest betrayals. No question for them of a knowledge of the Saviour by hearsay. That is why saints, unlike sinners, are never shocked.

Le pécheur est au coeur même de la chrétienté. It should give us new heart, not only for ourselves but for the world as a whole. For the world as a whole, whether it admits it or not, is the Christian world, is the world for which Christ died, the world in which the redemptive process is being worked out to its fulfilment, the world which travailleth even until now, so that it is wrong for us to despair. However great the mass of evil in the world it is wrong to despair: only if all struggle against that mass of evil had ceased would it be right to despair: and we know that in fact the struggle will not cease.

The First Sword

And Simeon said to Mary his Mother, Thy own
soul a sword shall pierce.   LK. II, 35

WE LIVE IN DAYS that are shadowed by fear. There are
the private, personal fears, as there always have been:
of pain, of illness, of death; of the loss of those we love,
of the coming of misfortune and tragedy to those we
love; but behind all these private fears there looms like
a sinister backcloth the despair and misery of the world
at large: the sense of foreboding, the feeling that disaster
is imminent and will not be averted. And because these
fears can make us gloomy and uncreative, robbing us of
our energy; can make us despair, forgetting God; it may
well follow that we for our part bring disaster nearer.
For despair invites it, being the will-to-death; only faith
and hope and love can combat it, being the will-to-life.
That is why fear, of any kind, is not something to be
simply escaped from and as far as possible forgotten,
but something to be faced, and understood, and transformed. And as in all our sorrows we can learn from
Mary's sorrows; so in all our fears we can learn from
Mary's fear.

Thy own soul a sword shall pierce. Simeon's words are not the first reference to fear in her life: at the very beginning of the story she is told, Fear not, as her destiny is announced to her, for indeed it is a destiny which must fill her heart with dread the more deeply she penetrates its meaning, the more clearly she begins to see what redemption must mean for herself and her Son, begins to see the shadows of the Cross closing in on him, and to understand what Evil will do to him. And yet, as we watch this life overcast by fears so immeasurably greater than ours, we are struck, not by any timidity or shrinking or sense of desperation, but by courage and strength and joy; and perhaps the courage and strength we can more readily understand, but how the joy? Yet she sings to Elizabeth of her joy at the things that are done in her; she is the mother, glad as she cuddles her child—divinely glad, for her divine child; she joins in the joys of the wedding at Cana; and though when she takes him once again on her lap when all is over it is only the heartbroken woman we are conscious of, still we are not to suppose that the *magnificat* was but the expression of a swiftly passing mood: the sword is always there, but so is the song. What is the secret of it?

The Church in its devotion to Mary lays great emphasis on the fact that in her motherhood she yet remained maiden as well; and we shall miss all the richness of this mystery if we think of this insistence as being purely or even primarily concerned with the physical. Motherhood produces fundamental psychological changes in a woman: it means normally the end of one life and the beginning of another; it means the loss of some qualities and the acquisition of others, a different mentality, a different outlook. The mother has known the deep experiences of love and joy, of pain and danger and sorrow: we think of her as the symbol of wisdom because she has known in her own body the mysteries of good and evil. The girl on the other hand is the symbol of opposite qualities: of a freshness and spontaneity and purity of heart which come precisely from inexperience, knowing only that reality can be ugly, not yet made wise through the lessons of sorrow: her courage, her strength, her wisdom, her joy, are from other sources. And in Mary alone, the Maiden-Mother, these opposite sets of qualities co-exist; it is this that gives her personality a richness which is unique; and it is because of this richness that she can teach us so much.

First of all we must see in her the twofold fear: the fear of the mother, based on the experience of known evil, the human ugliness which life has already revealed, as a mother feels her child's physical dangers in her own nerves and bones because she has already known them or their like in her own experience; the fear of the girl, sensing an evil that is all the more difficult to meet because it is unknown: sensed as an enemy because wholly alien, wholly unnatural; sensed as a danger in the way the evil presences and emanations of the ghost stories inspire in those who feel them the terror of the unknown.

Mary's life, then, is a song at once of innocence and of experience; and as this double richness means a double fear, so it means also a double love; and the love in its turn produces a double wisdom, a double trust, and therefore a double courage. *Mary pondered all these things in her heart:* it is her song of her experience, and the source of her mother-wisdom. She knew how he

17

that is mighty had done great things in her; she knew the overshadowing power of the Most High; she knew the gradually unfolding self-revelation of her Son; and knowing these things she could sense the Resurrection through the Cross, the joy through the pain, the triumph through the failure; and so she could find the courage to meet the sword. *Behold the handmaid of the Lord:* there, on the other hand, is her song of innocence: whatever may come it will be well, because it is his will, because he is Love: hers are eyes too that can look out untroubled on a future which is wholly veiled, simply because she has implicit trust in the God she loves, even before the trust has been justified by experience; and as the Mother can say, I can do all things in him who has strengthened me, so the Girl can say, I can do all things in him who will strengthen me.

But this love produces more than wisdom and trust and courage. We are told that love drives out fear: but it does not leave a vacuum behind it; it leaves joy in its place. Once assured of the ultimate outcome, the mother's fears are turned into joy because she can share in her son's ordeal, she can help, she is part of his vocation; the girl's fears are turned into the joy which is part of her pride in taking his life to herself. More than that, there is in each case the joy in a love which is itself a sustaining strength; and more than that again, the love that is strong enough to cast out fear is strong enough also to inspire that purely selfless joy in its object which is known to us selfish sinners far more in the relatively impersonal appreciation of the beauty of art than in the more personal and passionate appeal of human relationships; and as in Mary the Mother there is, unsullied by possessiveness, the mother's pride

18

and joy in her child, so in Mary the Maiden there is, unsullied by any self-regardingness, the girl's awe and joy in a Beauty and a Love whose infinite loveliness she can only adore.

What then must we do if we are to be freed from our fears? First of all we can try to imitate Mary the Mother. We can try to learn something of her wisdom. In prayer we can ponder God's power and God's pity: again and again, in the loosing of our sins, we have had experience of it: we need to deepen our awareness of that experience, so that the sense of the divine enfolding arms is always with us, and colours our judgments of immediate dangers and disasters, and helps us to see always, as she saw, the resurrection beyond the cross. So we shall come to have something of her trust in him who is mighty; and with her trust her courage; and with her courage her joy: a joy not merely from this divine sense of security but also, and more deeply, from the fact that, forgetting our own fears, we can share in his redeeming work as she shared in it, and perhaps even can know some faint stirrings of that yet diviner joy which is her selfless pride in her child.

But what of the wisdom of Mary the Maiden? How in our sinfulness can we hope ever to imitate that? How can we ever hope to recapture the qualities of a soul unravished by sin when sin in fact is so domiciled in our souls? We shall perhaps find an answer if we reflect that there is one kind of fear which is not something we need to be freed from but something we need to acquire. Mary could not but fear the Cross; but far more she feared the sin that caused the Cross. We for our part know all too well the misery of the world which is caused by the evil in the world; but of that

19

evil itself we have so little sense, so little dread; and so our own sinfulness goes to increase the weight of evil, and therefore in some sense the weight of misery. Could we have Mary's fear of sin we should reverse the process: the growing sense of sin would increase our sorrow, and therefore our love, and therefore our sense of the beauty and love and pity of God: and so we should share in the divine process of driving back the evil, of conquering the evil; and we should be helping to lessen not only the sin but the misery of the world.

But still the difficulty remains. In Mary the Mother there is the dread of sin based upon bitter experience: not of course in her own soul but in the souls of others, knowing the evil thing in itself, knowing its effects in misery and degradation and hatred and destruction; but in Mary the Maiden the dread is something quite different, as we have seen: the dread of something unknown, wholly alien, the dread of something sensed but not experienced as evil because unnatural, something from another, darker world; and so the question again presents itself: how are we to hope to imitate that? Can a soul recapture its lost innocence?

To study the lives of the saints who have once been sinners, is to be compelled to answer yes. It is not only the saints who have never gravely sinned, it is all the saints, who have about them precisely that quality of freshness, of youth of soul, of a simplicity so unlike the duplicities and complexities in which sin involves us, which we thought of as characterising the girl-symbol. With them as with us the experience is there, it lives on; but whereas it makes us old and seared and tawdry in heart, in them it is transmuted into something so different that sin becomes for them not an old and constant

20

companion whose every feature is familiar, but a fraud unmasked, an enemy revealed in his true colours, the alien of the virgin-saints seen and sensed as such. And how has this come about? Because sorrow for sin is creative: it has so increased their love of God, it has brought them so close to God, that they become like to God; and the man who is like to God is strange to sin.

It is not enough then to say that a growing sense of sin means a growing love of God and therefore a growing joy in God: we must say also that it means a growing closeness to God and therefore the recapturing of a primal innocence, with the special wisdom and strength and trust and joy which that innocence carries with it. And so it becomes quite clear what we must do if we would imitate Mary in her twofold richness of life. First to ponder these things in our hearts: to try to understand more deeply what God does to share in and cure man's sorrows and sins; and what we for our part have so differently done; and so to find true creative sorrow and the love and wisdom that spring from it. But then secondly to begin to say, Behold the handmaid of the Lord: and this is something we can say no matter what history of accumulated evil may lie behind, provided only that now we begin to know and acknowledge our nothingness and helplessness, and destroy all the self-fashioned and self-imposed masks we have presented to ourselves and to the world, and stand naked under the creative and re-creative hand of God. Be it done unto me: done from the very beginning, for there is nothing here but the negation of light and life; nothing therefore that can give any direction, have any rights, form any pattern; no power, no entity, no I, but only the dark chaos of a nothingness out of which God, but only God, can create a real man. Be it done unto me, then, in order that now at long last there may *be* an I, and all the old falsehoods and fictions of pride and vanity may be swept away; and so the new I is indeed something new, new-born, a beginning of life; and though the old experiences are there still, they begin to lose their power, they cease to be the driving force, to colour all the thoughts of the mind and the desires of the heart: we are become what St. Peter calls us, the first-born of creation, and in the fresh vivid light of the new dawn our eyes are opened and we see, see now with something of the vision of unsullied youth, see a new heaven and a new earth.

"The eyes of the saint make all beauty holy, and the hands of the saint consecrate everything they touch to the glory of God, and the saint is never offended by anything and is scandalised by no man's sin because he does not know sin. He knows nothing but the love and mercy of God, and he is here on earth to bring that love and that mercy to all men."[1]

How can he not be scandalised: How can he not know. Because now there is no common ground: there is no sin to call to sin, no abyss in him to answer the abysses of evil; sin has ceased to be connatural to him and is become alien like a foreign tongue.

---

[1] Thomas Merton: *Seeds of Contemplation.*

The Second Sword

And behold an angel of the Lord appeared in sleep to Joseph, saying: Arise, and take the child and his mother, and fly into Egypt: and be there until I shall tell thee. MT. II, 13

IN RECENT TIMES England has become a land of refuge for many exiles; Germans, Austrians, Jews, Poles, political refugees from many another country, all have found refuge in England and a home; and surely we may hope that their harbouring may bring upon us a blessing. In the Middle Ages men sought safety from pursuit in the sanctuary, the holy place; and the fact that men of to-day can find sanctuary in this country may help, we may hope, to make it itself a holy place in the end. But for them, though it means safety, it must still be *terra aliena*, a strange land: they have been uprooted, their own land and traditions and ways and possessions are lost to them, are left behind; and they know not only the poverty of dispossession but the sorrow of homesickness.

This Gospel scene of the flight into Egypt is like so many contemporary stories that it must seem particularly vivid to us. The night, the darkness, the sudden preparations and departure into the unknown, the strange, the perilous; and the parents, anxious for their

25

child's safety, and the Maiden-Mother with her double fears; and Egypt itself the symbolic land of darkness, of exile, of the prison camp: the whole story is a symbol, not of an adventure, a conquering of new territory, but of a loss.

The natural right to property is based upon a solid fact: that the human personality is not contained within the confines of the physical body. To be fully alive a man must have a setting. The personality is expressed and fulfilled through its extensions: through creative work, through human relationships, through home, through family roots and traditions, through the native soil and native land, and native culture. The word tradition means a handing on; it is a double process: a receiving from those who have gone before, a passing on to those who are to come; and where a tradition is really living it must in consequence change from generation to generation, it must be enriched by the thought and the labours of each succeeding age; and it is in that work of adapting and enriching a material environment that man's personality reaches its natural completion. That is why patriotism, the love of the *patria*—and we may take it here as including all that we mean by home —is a virtue: not nationalism, not enmity or pride or aggressiveness in regard to other nations, but a reverence and gratitude for the gifts that have come down to us, a love of our particular way of life and of the land in which the family tree is rooted and the family ways were begotten:

this little world,
This precious stone set in the silver sea . . .
This blessed plot, this earth, this realm, this England . . .

26

Yet it remains true that possessions, even these possessions, are a danger. Material property can imprison and enslave us; patriotism can degenerate into insularity and narrow-mindedness; the setting can become not an enlargement of personality but an encircling wall. That is why Christianity upholds the right to property but preaches at the same time the virtue of poverty of spirit. Life must have its dignity, and you must love the things that are worthy of love; but you must remain free. And sometimes the tyranny of material things can become so complete that it makes the love of God impossible: and either you must flee these things or you flee God. So it is that St. Thomas says of the flight into Egypt: *Voluit fugere ut fugientes a facie Dei revocaret:* He willed this flight that he might thereby bring back those who flee from the face of God: it is the symbol of that evangelical poverty, that giving up of material possessions, which is an assertion of the primacy of primary things.

Good living, comfort, pleasure, money, home, country: all these may, if we let them, become a flight from God: an attempt to forget him and his demands; and the more valuable they are in themselves, the more dangerous they may be to our self-deceiving minds:

> *I fled him down the nights and down the days;*
> *I fled him down the arches of the years;*
> *I fled him down the labyrinthine ways*
> *Of my own mind; and in the mist of tears*
> *I hid from him, and under running laughter—*

and sometimes it is a distraction unrealised for what it is until its empire is established, and sometimes it is a

27

way of forgetting which, consciously or unconsciously, we deliberately seek; in either case we find ourselves in the end enslaved.

We need then, in some form or other, a flight into Egypt to save us from idolatry and degradation. *Arise, and take the child:* and it was to be at once, and it was to be by night. That is poverty of spirit: to love the things that God has given you to complete your life, but to be ready to give them back to him if he requires them, and to give them at once: not grudgingly, not with reservations and grumblings, but readily, eagerly, if possible joyfully; and to give them back even though it is in the darkness, even though there seems no sense in it and the future is black and the world seems in consequence empty and cold.

Poor banished children of Eve, we call ourselves in the *Salve;* and there are moods, when the sun is shining and the earth is lovely and life is good, in which it seems very unreal; but the words are expressing not a mood but a fact. Our job is to live our life here as well as we can by doing God's will for us as well as we can: and that will includes many things that are lovely, which we must love; many joys which we must take gratefully and gladly from his hands; many things which are not transitory and fleeting but eternal, and will remain a part of us always; the knowledge and wisdom and love that life may bring us; but none the less it remains true that the setting as a whole, the material setting, is transitory, is fleeting, is not ultimately home. The human home that endures is not this house, this garden, these material things, but these human beings whom you love and the mutual love in which you all live and which makes you all a single entity.

28

Take the child and his mother, and be there until I shall tell thee: it is not only the going but the staying that God's will determines and that is part of our obedience. And that means two things. It means not clinging to good things when God requires them of us; it means also not being impatient to escape from bad things when God requires them of us. Egypt is the land of darkness. For some the sojourn in the darkness is a long one, perhaps seemingly an unending one; even the sunniest lives have their times of darkness: in either case these things have their purpose if only we can see it and welcome it: they are teaching us to be poor in spirit, they are teaching us not to be tyrannized over, they are teaching us to be free, they are teaching us the primacy of primary things, they are teaching us not to flee God who is our home.

But traditionally too the land of darkness is a land of peril, filled with evil powers and presences who seek to destroy. Sometimes it seems relatively easy to love God and to do his will, but there are the black moods, the times when the dark waters seem to be closing over us, we seem to turn inescapably to evil thoughts and things, we have a devil, the evil powers are abroad in the darkness. It is then that, unless we have learnt to be poor in spirit, the material world can turn on us and rend us, can drag us down and humiliate us, can blot out altogether the presence of God. For the black moods are in fact an uprising from the human underworld within us, an uprising which reduces—perhaps for a time almost to nothing—the power and authority of the spirit; and it is then especially that, unless we have really learnt to be poor in spirit, the material world can dominate and tyrannize over us, we can become the

29

slaves of our flesh, and the loveliness of God's earth can turn for us into an evil beauty like a lovely face ravaged by greed and cruelty and lust.

Here then especially we need to be prepared; but it is a preparation which must necessarily be a long process. We shall not become poor in spirit suddenly, when danger most acutely threatens. It is when God's yoke seems light and his presence near that we need to school ourselves to meet the darkness; and to school ourselves, not by occasional dramatic renunciations but by constant daily attention to his will in tiny things. *Seek ye first the kingdom of heaven:* if at every moment we consult his will for us, if when life's gracious things come to us we refer them back to him in gratitude and love, and when difficulties arise we turn to him also in obedience and love, then we are learning how to see the material world as his world and not ours, and material things as his gifts and not our creatures: and so we can hope to be able to obey, even though it must be done instantly, even though it must be in darkness, when the time comes for us to flee into Egypt in our turn.

But when Herod was dead, we are told, there again appeared an angel to Joseph in Egypt, saying: Arise, and take the child and his mother and go into the land of Israel: for they are dead that sought the life of the child. There is a striking parallelism of circumstance: again it is night, and Joseph asleep; and the words are almost identical; so that the similarity underlines the contrast: no longer question of a flight, but of a glad return, and the reason given: they are dead that sought the life of the child. Those who have learnt how to love the harshness as well as the tenderness of Love, to greet with gratitude the buffetings of God, come in the end to a state in which poverty of spirit is perfect in them, greed and possessiveness are dead in them: they are dead that sought the life of the child in them, the new-born of God, and so they are free to return. They are free to return to the world to love the world, to gather all God's creatures into the embrace of their love, because God's creatures can no longer endanger their love of God, they can only help to express it. So often the saints' lives follow this pattern: first the flight, the darkness, the searching for God; but then the return to the world of men, the search for men, the fulfilment of the love of God in the continuation of God's work for men. That is indeed the essence of Christian mysticism: that it can never be content with a solitary absorption in God on the mountain-top, unaware of the poor misguided worldlings who people the plains below; for the Word was made flesh and dwelt amongst us, and it is idle to say that you love God and are seeking God if you have no interest in the beings God loves so well that he made himself one of them in order to die for them. There are indeed the saints who are hermits and solitaries just as there are the saints who worked in the slums and hovels of the great cities; but all of them alike are fired by the same spirit, the same love; all of them alike share in Christ's redeeming care for the world.

And we who live in the plains, and who at best catch only the faintest echoes of the divine self-revealings which are given high above us, can we have any part in this rediscovery of the earth and this redeeming work? To all of us there must come sometimes, to most of us there will come often, the same command to leave our belongings, to leave something that we treas-

31

ure, and to go out into the darkness: not in any dramatic way, probably, this summons, but the small events we tend to think of as our share of life's misfortunes, missing their divine message. If we see them for what they really are, see them in the light of this divine abandonment of home *ut fugientes a facie Dei revocaret*, to bring back those who flee from God, then in us too they will gradually work a transformation; gradually they will lessen the hold of selfishness and greed upon our hearts; gradually they will make it more possible for us to love the things we like to think we love, and then perhaps to enlarge the boundaries of our love, to begin to love the things to which hitherto we had been indifferent or hostile; and so in the end, in our more pedestrian fashion, we shall be doing something of the same sort as the saints: we shall be learning to see the earth anew.

But this discovery of a new earth is not the final return, the final liberation. Still, so long as we are here, we remain the banished children of Eve: our home is elsewhere. And when we think of the flight into Egypt we should think not only of a time when we can be fit to return to earth, but of a time when we can be fit to enter heaven: we should pray not only for a love that is big enough to include the whole world, but for a love that is pure enough to meet God. For only then is the darkness really and fully over; only then is the exile ended, the day of the dark powers that sought our life really done: when God's mercy takes us to the land where darkness has no entrance, no dominion; the land where there is no loss, no sorrow, no homesickness, but only the light and wonder of the eternal Presence, the glory and gaiety and peace of God.

The Third Sword

And not finding him, they returned into
Jerusalem, seeking him.　　　　　LK. II, 45

THERE IS a mysterious element in this story of the loss
of the child Jesus in Jerusalem which at first sight is
very baffling. They go up to the city for the festival
with their kinsfolk and acquaintance; the feast over, the
caravan starts out on the return journey; Jesus, now a
boy of twelve, is left considerable freedom, and it is not
till the night that his parents realise that he is not with
the pilgrimage. They hurry back to Jerusalem, dread
in their hearts; they find him in the Temple, listening
to the doctors of the law and asking them questions—
a not unusual scene, except for the astonishing wisdom
of his words—and then, when his mother gently re-
proaches him, he offers no word of apology for the distress he has caused them, hardly a word that could be
called an explanation, since they fail to understand what
he says to them. How could he seem so callous?

His words affirm his divine sonship: there are claims
upon him far more exalted and far more demanding
than theirs. But the whole scene, also, is a revelation of

35

divinity: the story goes on to tell us how he went back with them and was subject to them, and yet here there is a sense of detachment which seems harsh and callous because he is not only Mary's child but Mary's God, and God has austere lessons to teach. Later on he was to feel abandoned by his Father on the Cross: it was an essential part of his work on earth, his sacrifice; and she who is to share so closely in that work and that sacrifice must experience something of the same thing: the lesson must be learnt. Certainly it was not learnt immediately; you imagine her telling the story so many years later, looking back down the years to those far-off dream-like days of his childhood: they understood not the word that was spoken to them, she says; but she kept all these things in her heart, till in the end they became clear: and what was the lesson she finally learnt?

In the last chapter we were thinking of our attitude to things; here we are led to think of our attitude to persons. The love of material things can be merely greed and possessiveness, the lust for pleasure or profit or power; but the love of human beings can be these things also, and then it is not real love at all, though we may deceive ourselves into thinking it to be. Because of our selfishness, to love in this real and deep sense is not an easy thing, not something given, but a hard thing, a thing that we have to learn, to create. First to love God; then to love others as coming from him, as given us by him, as his other children: this is what we have to learn if we are really to love. Here more than anywhere, greed and possessiveness turn beauty into ugliness and light into darkness.

For a human being is more valuable than all the

things that the world contains put together; and it is by that that we can measure our responsibility towards him. We are like children stumbling in the dark; and if God in his tenderness gives us another of his children to companion and comfort and help us we must cherish the gift more than all riches, but we must know the heaviness of our responsibility: we must be always at pains to keep it in God's sight and God's care.

We need human love to help us on our way; but three things will destroy it and leave us bereft and lonely, and they are things to which we are very prone.

Greed will destroy it: greed which means loving persons for the sake of things, loving human beings only for what they can give us. It is Satan who offers things to Christ in the temptation: God offers not things but himself. He asked the two disciples, What seek ye? and they answered him, Where dwellest thou?—they wanted not a what but a who. It is the same when Christ says to St. Thomas Aquinas, Thou hast written well of me, Thomas; what reward wouldst thou have of me? and he answers, *Nihil nisi Te, Domine:* Nothing, Lord, save thyself. It is easy indeed to see that this is the right scale of values; it is not always easy to act on it. Greed lies deep down in us; and it can assume forms, it can hide behind appearances, which easily deceive us and others too. Of course I love you: I would do anything in the world for you, we say: yes, but why? Sometimes giving can be a form simply of pleasure-seeking, of self-indulgence. I am only trying to show you how I love you, we say; when really we are snatching at a purely selfish sensuality of our own. Look at all the things I have given you and done for you, we say: not realising that it was simply because it gave us pleasure, or even—poor fools that we are—because it ministered to a sense of power. Command that these stones be made bread: but you cannot turn greed into the bread of love if the motive that drives you is itself greed; you can do it only by learning to love and obey every word that proceedeth from the mouth of God.

Greed is selfishness grasping at what one desires; possessiveness is selfishness clinging to what one has; and each of them equally can destroy love. Motherhood is for us the symbol of a perfect because a perfectly selfless love; but its very perfection makes the travesties of it the more terrible. Think of the possessive mother, clinging to her children long after the time has come for them to be independent, retarding their development, frustrating their careers, preventing them from marrying: she is not loving at all, she is destroying the personalities she pretends to love. But the same can be true of wives and husbands; the same can be true of friends; wherever there is the desire to dominate, to mould and fashion according to one's own ideas, wherever demands are absolute and unconditional, there is not love but destruction. Human love can never be unconditional: in all things we are only stewards, and here more than anywhere we are only stewards. Our model here especially must be Mary the true mother: her whole vocation consisting in living for his vocation: mothering him in his childhood, looking after him in his youth, and then, when her work for the time being is done and he is ready for his public life, withdrawing quietly into the background until she is needed again to sustain him in his Passion.

But a third thing too can kill love; and it is idolatry. If you exalt the objects of your love until your picture is a false one; if you idealise them; if you project upon them your own ideal picture of your own ideal self; then you are loving not a real person but a dream. The result is inevitable: sooner or later the difference between ideal and real obtrudes itself upon you; then you feel disappointed, cheated, you feel quite unjustly that you have somehow been wronged; and so, what looked to you like love but never was turns to dislike: the unreal romance is over before it ever touched reality, and real love is still as remote from your heart as ever. . . . What we need is real love of real people, to heal our loneliness; and that means seeing them as they really are, and loving that; and that in its turn means not worshipping them as flawless ideals and deities, but helping them, and being helped by them, to worship God. More than that, as long as a fictitious idealised love dominates your heart it tends to exclude everything else: it is jealous, possessive, absorbing, greedy; and because the fiction is so largely a self-projection, it tends to make you more and more of an egoist. It is not until you are finding not the sham love but the real that you can begin to learn the austere but grand and essential lesson: that it is not just one being that you must love but all beings: you must love all life. Perhaps, in order to learn that lesson properly, we sometimes need the hard schooling of disappointment and loneliness; and so God gives it to us as he gave it to Mary and Joseph. He was to know utter loneliness in the garden and on the Cross; she must learn it now as she seeks him sorrowing; and she must learn it in order to fulfill the second and crowning part of her destiny, to be the mother of all men.

But the universality of charity is not something confined to her, it is something enjoined on every Christian: we need the same lesson in our turn. So disappointment comes to us with a purpose: separation, the loss of love, the death of one we love or the death of love itself; and it is then that we have to try not to grumble or rebel, but to learn from what is being done in us. For we shall never love all beings unless we love God more than all beings—not necessarily with a greater emotional intensity, but with a greater loyalty of will. God is said to be a jealous God, not because he will not allow us to have other loves, but because he will not have rivals. And if in fact we love other things in defiance of him, or away from him, as distractions from him, then our love tends to turn sour and in the end to destroy itself. So again, as with material things, we need poverty of spirit; not in order that, where creatures are concerned, we may love less, or less intensely, but that our love may be real. The love of God, once again, is a question essentially not of emotion but of devotion of the will: to love God more than anything else means essentially to love his will, effectively, more than any claim of any creature. Love with your whole heart; but make sure that your heart is given to God: then you are giving the one you love something greater than a purely human love: you are giving a love which is indwelt by God: you are loving not only with your own love, but with God's.

He was twelve years old: we are given this lesson by Christ the Boy. It is a pity that nowadays, while Christianity has at Christmas its devotion to the infancy

40

of Christ and always its devotion to the Christ-Man, the redeemer, the devotion to the youthful Christ, the *Puer Aeternus,* is so largely lost. Youth has lovely qualities. It has a freshness and charm, a shy grace, a clarity of vision, a sincerity, that later years can never recapture. But it has something else:

"the thoughts of youth are long, long thoughts"; there is a quality also of remoteness, as though the attention were half directed to some world unseen, the heart in some way withdrawn from the immediate phenomenal world even though then, coming back to it, it seems to give it something of its own urgent vitality. So it is the Boy-Christ who teaches his mother to realise, This child is not mine but God's; teaches us in our turn to say of all those we love, These are not mine but God's. The first essential is that, like Christ in the Temple, we should be near to the Father; the second, that with those we love we should together be near the Father; for only so can we find freedom from greed and possessiveness and idolatry. When we are babies we need other human beings all the time to look after us; and again when we are grown up we need other human beings, and know our need; it is boyhood that is independent. And so we need the lesson of Christ the Boy, not to give us back a natural independence of temperament and heart which is not proper to manhood, but to show us the supernatural counterpart of it, to touch creatures very gently lest we destroy them and ourselves.

Mary kept all these things in her heart, until the lesson became clear in the fullness of her wisdom. It is for us to ask her to give us a share in that wisdom; for her motherhood of men, her concern for all men, is certainly something in which we are called to share, and if we lack it we shall only harm those we try to cherish.

There is one final lesson. They sought him sorrowing, but in the end they found him; after three days they found him. It is like the three days in the tomb. Three days of darkness, but then the light; three days of death, but then the resurrection. At first sight you would say that this lesson taught by the Boy Christ is a purely harsh and austere one; but that is not its ending. In the end it tells us: though for long days and months and years you seem to be bereft of God, to have lost God, seem in vain to have sought him sorrowing, still you must be of good heart: the search will not be in vain in the end. *They found him . . . and he went down with them, and came to Nazareth.* As with human love so with divine love there is first the lesson to be learnt—the loneliness, the disappointments, the sorrow that can teach us not to be greedy—but then there is the union, the companionship, that nothing can shatter, that even death cannot dissolve. For long years perhaps the desert; but then the joy of Nazareth, the House of Bread—and the breaking of bread together is the symbol of all the warmth and hospitality of home. So here in the Temple he is saying in effect as he said explicitly later on: Seek and ye shall find; and when after all the trials and discouragements you are ready at last to love him you will find him, and he will go down with you as he went down with them, to Nazareth, and will give you in full measure, as he gave them, and everlastingly, his companionship, and joy, and peace.

The Fourth Sword

Go forth, ye daughters of Sion, and see the king in the diadem wherewith his mother crowned him in the day of his espousals. CANT. III, 11

THE WAY to Golgotha lies through the narrow, torrid, dusty streets of the city; you think of the jostling, jeering crowd, the noise and the tumult; and then in the midst of it all it is as though a silence falls as he meets his mother: a private silence for these two alone as everything else is blotted out and they are conscious only of each other. (That concentration of gaze, that rapt and exclusive attention, is what our daily prayer ought to be.) They cannot speak, and so their sorrow is the greater; and for Mary it is a double sorrow: the mother's sorrow, watching the torments of the son her body bore, and the girl's sorrow, flinching from the revelation of naked evil and cruelty destroying innocence and beauty and love. A double sorrow, but yet she is silent; it is not for her to find an emotional outlet for her grief, for she is here because of him: she is here to fulfil her vocation as mother by helping him to fulfil his: she is here to crown him in the day of his espousals to the sorrows of man.

There is a sharp contrast here between his mother and the women of Jerusalem to whom he spoke: and the contrast is in the fact that he spoke. They loved him and sorrowed for him, but their sorrow seems too noisy, as though there is an element of self-pity in it, as though they are in fact calling attention to themselves, and instead of consoling him they look to him to console them. In her is the silence of strength, and so she can give him the strength of her silence: it is what she is there to do. In her there are the two contradictory agonies: the longing to save him from his unbearable agony, the effort to help him to finish his work; and it is the second that she must do, giving him to the world on the cross as she has given him to the world in the stable.

That is the first thing that Mary shows us. If her heart had been filled with a soft sentimental pity she would not have helped but have hindered. Human love helps when it is within the framework of vocation, when it expresses the will of God. A mother's vocation is fulfilled when she offers her son to God, to life, to his own destiny; ruined when she clings to him for her own sake on the plea of saving him from hurt. *Go forth and see the king in the diadem wherewith his mother crowned him:* and this is the crowning, her offering of her son to the Father, her strengthening of her son for the kingship of the cross.

For the very offering is itself a help to him, comforting and gladdening him. For her, the meeting can be only agony: and John and Magdalen must have tried to restrain her, but she insisting, I must be with my

46

son, he will have need of me. And so she shows us a second thing: we are not merely to avoid confusing true pity with sentimental pity, we are to keep clear the distinction between true pity and self-pity. We for our part are not often asked to shoulder very heavy crosses perhaps; but the small ones come our way, and they fill us with self-pity, they make us yearn for, and expect, and perhaps demand, sympathy till in the end we make others miserable in their turn: it is then that we should think of this scene, compare our noisy lamentations with this silence, our emotional wallowings with this strength, our wasted opportunity with this glory. He had need of her; he has need, St. Paul tells us, of us too. At Mass the priest raises the chalice in offering to God, and with it the lives, the work, the joys and pains, of his people: and similarly in every moment of trouble there is the material not of self-pity but of self-offering as a part of Christ's offering: not only a completion now of his work, but a lightening then of his load. It was not only Simon of Cyrene who eased the weight from his shoulders: it was all those from his mother onwards, all those then present and those to come, whose love consoled and strengthened him. To turn a small trial into a trough of self-pity is to make it and ourselves still more petty; to share it thus with him is to turn it, however small it may be, into a thing of grandeur, a giving of life.

And in Simon there is a further lesson for us. They *constrained* one Simon of Cyrene. . . . He was not eager to help; he hated the idea of helping; but he was forced; and what followed then? Christ had said, My yoke is sweet and my burden light; he had said when the woman touched his garment, Virtue hath gone out from

47

me. It is unthinkable that virtue did not go out also from the wood's touch; and that Simon having begun in reluctance did not end in joy, finding the wood sweet indeed and the burden light. Good people are so often worried and distressed because, they say, they feel no devotion, they feel no love of God in their hearts, no readiness to suffer anything for him, no zest for sacrifice. Then they have to be told, feelings are of no account: devotion is a question not of feelings but of will.

True, the emotions can be a great strengthening for the will: you work better when you are emotionally full of zest for the work; you work with more energy when you are gay and sanguine and your heart is in it; and there are times when God gives the emotional zest in his service to show us that his burden is light and to help us to form the habit of working for him with vigour and constancy. But if he takes the joy away and gives us fatigue and boredom; if our hearts feel dead within us; if everything connected with his service seems purposeless and futile and perhaps cruel: provided we go on with the thing to be done have we cause for despair or depression? On the contrary, it is then that we can show, and know, that we really are devoted: it is then that we can show, and know, that it is really God we love and not his gifts, and that love, for that very reason, can grow to its perfection; for love and devotion are not in the emotions but in the will.

Devotion, St. Thomas tells us, means the will to give oneself readily to God's service; and he goes on to show how devotion and love are reciprocal causes; charity causing devotion, since love makes one ready to

48

serve one's friend, and devotion feeding charity, since friendly deeds safeguard and deepen friendship. Whenever, then, you in fact do what God tells you, you are growing in the love of God, no matter what your feelings may be. Fill the water-pots with water; and they filled them to the brim: that is the only thing that matters, they did what they were told, they filled the water-pots, and they did it thoroughly, they filled them to the brim. And so the water was changed into wine; and so Simon's reluctance was turned into joy in the end; and so every act of obedience, however dry or dead the heart may feel, safeguards and deepens love in the soul.

But good people worry again because they say, I never become any better; I go on week after week and year after year committing the same sins, being equally unsuccessful at my attempts at prayer, never apparently becoming any less selfish, never apparently drawing any nearer to God. . . . Are they so sure? What they ought to ask themselves is, Do I equally go on week after week and year after year doing the same hard things for God, keeping for his sake the many other commandments that are often hard for me, going doggedly on trying to pray, going doggedly on trying to help other people? And if the answer is yes, as it is, then they should know that whatever the surface appearances and disappointments, love is growing within them. We live our lives at many different levels; and the events on the surface we can see and assess, but we may know little or nothing of what is going on deep down beneath the surface. If nature has made you choleric you will no doubt go on losing your temper; if nature has made you lethargic you will no doubt go on being lazy—what do these things matter if at the same time charity is being fed in your soul by devotion, as friendship is safeguarded and deepened by friendly deeds?

They constrained one Simon of Cyrene—and perhaps God sometimes constrains those who love him but think they do not love him, so that in the doing of the work, the bearing of the cross he gives them, their love may grow and deepen though they remain unaware of it, till in the end they find that beneath the apparent dryness and sterility great things have been going forward in them and holiness has been born.

But it is not only God's cross that we are called to share with them, but those of his other children too; and here also the same thing applies. The question is not whether we are emotionally eager to help (though if at any time we are it is a great gift), but whether in fact we do help. And in the last resort these crosses are all the one cross: to help other men, out of charity, is to help God in his agony; and to help God is to help the race of men. So it is that even the smallest action of this sort can have a cosmic significance: and wherever in the midst of the noise and heat and bustle of the world there falls a moment of silent sympathy, the giving of comfort and strength for the doing of God's will, there the redemption is operative and the wounds of the world are being healed.

Till the day break and the shadows retire—we read in the Song of Songs—I will go to the mountain of myrrh and to the hill of frankincense: myrrh for his burial, the myrrh the Magi brought; and on that final journey into the darkness his mother remained with him, companioning him all the way, staying with him till the end. And before the daybreak there must be the heart-break; but the daybreak came, the dawn of resurrection; and then the sorrows that had gone before remained only as the material of the new and never-ending joy. So it can be with all his followers in their turn: to take up as readily, as devotedly as possible the crosses he sends, to bear them with him and for him, and to go on unflaggingly till the day break and the shadows retire, to go on if necessary even to the mountain of myrrh, to the darkness and the burial: that is the way to know in the end something of the joy that flooded, so inexplicably, the soul of Simon; to know something of that far greater and more inexpressible joy of that other, later, meeting of son and mother, when the day indeed had broken, the dawn indeed had come, and there was only joy for them now and the shared happiness of their love, the love that, having gone down in silence together to the very depths of human agony, now rose together to the heights of more than human glory, to that joy of which no tongue can tell, but which is promised in degree in God's mercy to all those who, in company with Mary, try to love and follow and serve her son.

The Fifth Sword

When Jesus therefore had seen his mother and the disciple standing whom he loved, he saith to his mother: Woman, behold thy son.   JN. XIX, 26

WHEN A hurt or a sorrow, a loss or a cross, is stated in words, the words seem to make the facts more real and more cruel, more hard to bear: there is a flat finality about them—I am going away; I don't love you; She is dead—that is like the tolling of a knell in the mind and heart. Mary had been standing afar off; but now she drew near; and would he now at the end have a word to speak to his mother?

Yes, and it was concerned with her comfort, his friend's care of her; yet at the same time it drove the sword deeper because it drew her life with him to a close: he was leaving her.

And yet this word of dereliction for her has at the same time been taken throughout the ages as the symbol for the grand, universal, enlargement of her vocation as mother: her motherhood of men. Woman, behold thy son John: but with him also the whole race of men, thy sons because my brothers. And her work

55

now will be to care for and cherish them as she had cared for and cherished him; to help them to fulfil their vocations as she had helped him fulfil his.

Yet it might well seem that this was not the moment for new glories and new responsibilities, this hour of her final dereliction. Why should it not rather have been at Pentecost, when the Church was established by the indwelling of the Spirit, and her own special work within the Church's life might therefore be thought to have formally begun? Perhaps the answer is simply that she for her part had no need to wait, as the apostles needed to wait: she had already now—and this moment was the final consummating lesson—all the knowledge and experience she needed. But there is something more. Here, at this moment, she is stripped of all human resources, and thrown back entirely upon God. Later, John will be there to help her, others will be there to help her; no one can help her at this moment when she has eyes only for her dying son. All ye who pass by the way, attend and see if there be any sorrow like to my sorrow: there is no prop, no help, no comfort that can have any meaning. And in the fact that it is indeed at that moment of utter negation that this universal motherhood is given to her there is a great lesson for us.

When prayer seems most hopeless it may well be most fruitful; when the search for God and the attempt to love God seem most futile and barren they may well be most creative: Why? Because if then we turn to God in humility, knowing our failure, we make it possible for him to work in us, and under his creative touch the soul comes to life, the flame is kindled, even though we remain unconscious of it. Whereas at other times our efforts may in fact be egoistic and self-reliant, or greedy of reward, and then we fail, however convinced we may be of our success. "A man," writes Thomas Merton, "who is not stripped and poor and naked within his own soul will always unconsciously do the works he has to do for his own sake rather than for the glory of God. He will be virtuous not because he loves God's will but because he wants to admire his own virtues. But every moment of the day will bring him some frustration that will make him bitter and impatient, and in his impatience he will be discovered. To say that I am made in the image of God is to say, that love is the reason for my existence; for God is love. Love is my true identity. Selflessness is my true self. Love is my true character. Love is my name. I who am without love cannot become love unless Love identifies me with himself. But if he sends his own love, himself, to act and love in me and in all that I do, then I shall be transformed, I shall discover who I am and shall possess my true identity by losing myself in him. And that is what is called sanctity."

When at the end we see our lives for what they really are, see them against the pure light of eternity, shall we see them as largely a sham Christianity, perhaps more or less respectable, law-abiding, kindly, but really, underneath, always clinging to the self-will which is the root of evil, our very piety coloured by our pride? Or shall we be able to say that in spite of all our sin we did try to make God the master in everything, did try to love his will in everything even though we constantly failed, did try to take the "leap in the dark" and tumble our lives into his hands as a total gift? That at any rate is the one essential thing we have to do. He that loseth his life shall find it. With us as with Christ, first the death and only then the resurrection; with us as with Mary, first the nakedness and dereliction of spirit, and only then the flowering of the divine vocation.

How is it to be done? We have to go down into his death: we have to go down into the darkness within us, recognise the evil within us, the pride and the egoism, and recognise how they colour and taint all the things that we do, and how powerless we are to turn the darkness into light—there is only one thing, says St. Thomas, of which man is the first cause: it is evil—and then in the nakedness of that self-knowledge we can give ourselves wholly into the hands of the Spirit and the Spirit can recreate us, for in the death of pride and egoism the soul is reborn as a child.

Maritain has some wise words on the parables of the man counting his resources before building a tower, the king counting his army before meeting his enemy in the field: "Which means to say," he writes, "before setting to work for God and to fight against the devil, first calculate your forces; and if you consider yourself well enough equipped to begin, you are a fool, because the tower to be built costs an outrageous price, and the enemy coming out to meet you is an angel, before whom you are of no account. Get to know yourself so well that you cannot contemplate yourself without flinching. Then there will be room for hope. In the sure knowledge that you are obliged to do the impossible, and that you can do the impossible in him who strengthens you, then you are ready for a task which can be performed only through the Cross."[1]

So, at times, God takes away all props, all help, from his children; leaves them apparently bereft; reduces them apparently to failure and desolation, so that some-

58

times they seem to have no faith left in him, in themselves, in anything at all: but it is all done with a purpose, with this purpose, for when at last there is nothing left but dry bones, then, if they turn to him in humility, he can make the dry bones live, and bring success out of failure, and hope and achievement out of despair. "And he said to me: Prophesy concerning these bones; and say to them: Ye dry bones, hear the word of the Lord. . . .Behold I will send spirit into you and you shall live. And I will lay sinews upon you, and will cause flesh to grow over you, and will cover you with skin: and I will give you spirit and you shall live, and you shall know that I am the Lord." [1]

When failure comes upon us, when we are tempted to depression or despair, it is of these dry bones that we should think; and see whether in fact there is some work waiting to be done for God, and turn to him, and beg him to work in us in spite of our frailties and failures; and so in us, as in their greater ways in the saints, the failures and the frustrations become creative.

But there is here a perennial difficulty which confronts many of us if we try to put all this into effect: we have to confess to ourselves a lack of will, we cannot even bring ourselves to will to begin on what needs to be done. In other words, we cannot conquer our sloth. We must of course be sure that we are not confusing sloth with physical or mental fatigue, with nerve-strain, with laziness or indolence. Devotion means the will to give oneself readily to God's service; sloth means a refusal or perhaps more accurately a culpable inability to achieve the will to give oneself readily to his service. A culpable inability: this is the noonday demon of the

---

[1] Ezechiel xxxvii, 4-6.

psalm: the boredom, the lack of volition, that assails one in the afternoon of the day or the afternoon of life, the middle-day, the middle-years, or again that marks that second stage in God's service when the freshness and lyricism have gone, the emotional enthusiasm is a thing of the past, and what was once easy and exciting and rewarding is now nothing but a hard grind, a clinging to God and his work only with "naked intent of the will." How then can we turn to him in our failures if we lack the will to turn? How can we take him our failures and frustrations if we lack the will to go to him at all?

Perhaps in this scene at the foot of the cross a double answer is given us. There must surely be, first of all, in Mary that same unbreakable concentration of attention that we saw on the road to Calvary. There was also, in the second place, the giving of this new duty, this new work: the mothering of humanity.

The concentration of gaze: we should not be slothful if we lived habitually and familiarly in his presence. If we refused to live on the surface of life, to float placidly in the conventionalised religious shallows: if we freed ourselves, at whatever cost, from the frenzied tempo of modern life and taught ourselves to be still, to pray; then, in that prayer-stillness we should begin to be aware of the distant horizons which give this world its meaning, and so to do the work of every day in God and with God and for God; and his companion-ship would vitalise our wills and liberate us from our sloth.

But then there is also the work for humanity. It is more difficult, as St. John pointed out, for a man to love God whom he seeth not than to love his brother whom he seeth. But to be spurred to one kind of initiative and activity is to find it easier to embark on others. (It is of course possible to make activity in the world, even the most beneficent, consciously or unconsciously a screen, an escape, from the presence of God: but it need not be so.) In these days it is hardly possible for anyone to remain unaware of the desperate needs of the world; but to the Christian these needs must appear in an especially forcible and dramatic form. For Christianity points us through death to life, through darkness to light; but it would seem as though the world to-day were facing in exactly the opposite direction, as though deep down within there were the will-to-death, as though the world were dying because it wants to die.

Sometimes indeed you find this death-wish explicit and complete, expressed in individual—or race—suicide. More often you find it in a paralysis of the will, a despair which destroys initiative; and there is an expression of this in the breakdown of the structure and machinery of society, a breakdown which goes very deep, so that the attempt to stem it by frenzied legislation and short-term policies is but tinkering; there is an expression of it too in the passive acceptance of encroaching totalitarianism; and there is an expression of it in the hatred of beauty and wisdom and all the things that bring life to the spirit. All these things are simply a cry to the dark gods of destruction, Crucify us, crucify us; and why is there this adoration of death? We know in our own lives that in so far as we give ourselves to pride and falsehood, cruelty and greed, we call down death and disintegration upon ourselves; but there is that in us which lusts after that disintegration, and it will conquer us unless we learn that life is to be found

61

not in self-worship but in Love-worship, that our name is love. So it is with a society which refuses that lesson: it may go on perhaps for centuries living on the surface forgetting the deep places, content without God; but sooner or later the shell cracks, the hollowness is revealed, and there is nothing left but the mocking grin of despair.

But what if we ourselves, despite our Christianity, are in the same position? We must go back to this same scene on Calvary, and see again God's self-revelation there. Jerusalem, Jerusalem, he had said once before, thou that stonest the prophets and killest them that are sent to thee, how often would I have gathered thy children as the hen doth gather her chickens under her wing, and thou wouldest not. God's love is far greater than any human categories; and his fatherhood does not exclude those qualities we associate more especially with motherhood: the gentleness, the tenderness, the intuitive understanding and sympathy. There are men who have to be in fact both father and mother to their motherless children; and sometimes they do in fact develop these other qualities, and in so doing give us a clue to what the love of God in its fullness means. And here again, at the foot of the Cross, the same fact is taught us in the bestowal upon us of his own mother: it is God saying, in effect, You can come to me like that, as to a mother.

And so the first lesson is deepened and reinforced: we cannot let ourselves be desperate and despondent, because we must be conscious of God's enfolding arms, God's motherly care and understanding and sympathy. We know that God's wisdom will send trials and derelictions; but in the light of this lesson we know that they are sent only to be creative for us and in us; and that just as out of Mary's dereliction came this greatness and this glory, so too, out of our small tribulations can come in our small way a sharing in her work: an ability to have something of her wise and tender and perceptive care for the people or the things God gives us to cherish.

For us then only to try to take them when they come without bitterness, without gloom, as a way in which our egoism can be exorcised, our hearts liberated to live in God and share God's power. And then too we shall know in the end of the joy of the final outcome. A woman when she is in labour hath sorrow because her hour is come; but when she hath brought forth the child she remembereth not the anguish, for joy that a man is born into the world. Mary had brought him forth into life, and now on Golgotha she watched over his death, his journey into the other greater life, and soon her sorrow too would be turned into greater joy. So for us too, if only we have faith and courage enough: You now have sorrow, but I will see you again and your heart shall rejoice; and your joy no man shall take from you.

The Sixth Sword

*And Respha the daughter of Aia took haircloth
and spread it under her upon the rock from the
beginning of the harvest till water dropped upon
them out of heaven; and suffered neither the
birds to tear them by day nor the beasts by night.*

II KINGS, XXI, 10

THE PIETA, God's mother holding her dead son in her
arms, is a symbol of the self-imposed powerlessness of
God in the hands of men. Christ's body was still divine
in death as it is divine in life: divine, yet robbed of all
its human, natural, powers: taken down from the cross
by the soldiers, held in Mary's arms, wrapped by Joseph
of Arimathea in the linen cloth, carried to burial. In the
Mass too God makes himself a passive thing, to be held
and moved and broken by the fingers of the priest; and
you see that powerlessness most appallingly manifest in
the black mass of the satanists. But to every human being God gives a similar terrifying power over himself:
the power to reject him if he will. Power is a common-
place, and to some an attractive, thing; yet how terrifying also when we reflect upon it. A man has power
over himself, over other men, over other creatures,
over God himself: he has power, in small ways or in
great, to change history; he has power to save or ruin
souls.

67

The Pietà is the symbol of God's love. If none of his creatures had free-will, what a neat and tidy place the world would be: all things joining together in an unsullied song of praise to God; no problem of evil, no problem of pain, no problem of hell, no hatred. No hatred; but also no love, no friendship: and it was love and friendship that God wanted most of his creation; it was to make love possible that he gave some of his creatures freedom.

The terrible choice is given. You can put power at the service of love; and then it is creative and beneficent and lovely, as it is in God. Or you can divorce power from love; and then it becomes destructive, evil, ugly. Jacob Boehme indeed held that such a divorce of power from love is in fact the root evil; and we may well agree with him, we who have seen power in complete corruption, with all its tyranny and ruthlessness and cruelty and dark malignance. This does indeed follow inescapably from the first primordial sin of pride: the refusal to obey is itself a determination to exercise power autonomously, independently of God; but if independently of God, then independently of love. And so man's paternal dominion over the world, his family, was lost to him. And the darkest pages in the world's history, and in the Church's history, are those which tell of the horrible effects of man's lust for power and abuse of power.

It is easy to use power over others irresponsibly: for the pleasure or prestige or self-aggrandizement to be found in its exercise. It is easy to use it selfishly: turning people into means instead of ends, means to our own profit, our own good, instead of ourselves setting out to achieve theirs. There may be a temptation to use it cruelly, for the dark pleasure that cruelty itself gives; or with that particular sort of inhumanity which puts more store on patterns than on persons, on the neatness and efficiency of a scheme instead of on the uniqueness of every individual soul. Power, in this sense of authority, corrupts whenever it turns to possessiveness, to jealousy, to petty tyrannies, to officiousness, to impersonality; and it corrupts for the same reason, that it is divorced from love.

It is the same with other forms of power. There is mental power: the cleverness that can be used for vanity for the discomfiture of others, for the perversion of truth, the destruction of souls; the critical faculty that can be used proudly, rashly, destructively; the wit that can turn to cruelty. There is the power given by those personal qualities—charm, beauty, attractiveness—which engender love, and therefore vulnerability, in others; and which again can be used so irresponsibly, so heartlessly, so cruelly.

All power implies a corresponding responsibility; and the greater the power the greater the responsibility because the greater the danger. And so we come back to the Pietà; for the greatest and most terrible of all powers is this power that God himself gives us, to love him or hurt him. One of the fearful things about power is that we cannot measure the effect of the abuse of it: if we wantonly hurt other human beings we know that evil will come of it, but we cannot foretell the extent of the evil. If we wantonly hurt God we can only suppose that the resultant evil must be immeasurably magnified: it is the whole purpose of creation that we are then attempting to frustrate, since we are refusing to God the primary purpose of his creation of man.

And because he has told us clearly that to sin against his creatures is to sin against himself, we must see all abuse of power in this light, as taking on something of the character of this evil; and so we cannot be indifferent to the smallest manifestation of it.

Yet the power is given us; we cannot be rid of it. Authority has to be exercised; personal gifts have to be used: how can we attempt to make sure that our use of power will not in fact be an abuse? Only by making ourselves powerless before God, as the dead body of Christ was powerless; only by becoming "stripped and poor and naked" within our own souls, so that the Spirit can invest us with his divine power and transform our impulses and cure our pride.

We live in an age of power. The vast resources which science puts at man's disposal are paralleled by the mighty concentrations of economic and political power which characterise our world. But on the other hand, there are thinkers who look now to the coming, out of our present chaos, of a new age in the world, an age of the Spirit, an age of inwardness in which men, turning again to contemplation, turning away from the frenzied pursuit of superficial ends and opening their hearts to the indwelling of the Spirit, the indwelling of love, will bring about a deep revolution in our ways of thought and the ways of life. For just as at the first Pentecost the coming of the Spirit into the hearts of the apostles was the crowning and consummation of the work and sacrifice of the God-Man—that inward possession completing the outward teaching and example and redemption which was the mission of the Son—so now the renewed, redoubled activity of the Spirit in the Church and in the world would complete that re-

demptive work in the world by internalising all that the Christian centuries have achieved in fashioning, defining, elucidating, the Christian way of life: a great upsurge of charity throughout the world, so that power would go forth from men as it went forth from Christ, not through the words they speak but through the love in their hearts; God's law no longer something heard and if possible obeyed as an external ruling, but something deep within them, the rhythm of their hearts.

Certainly it is when you find men like that that you find power purely beneficent; and if the age of power is not to go down into utter destruction it must learn the way to this other and greater power: the power which flung the apostles out of their hiding and into the streets to preach the wonderful works of God, the power that invested the Roman girl-saints and their followers in other ages and led them to defy the might and cruelty of secular tyranny, the power that has possessed all those who have sacrificed themselves for the good of humanity. Secular power may possibly unify a world through force; only love can unite a world in freedom.

You call me Master, and Lord; and you say well, for so I am. If then I, being your Lord and Master, have washed your feet; you also ought to wash one another's feet. For I have given you an example, that as I have done to you, so you do also. The pattern is there, the way power is to be used: not in arrogance and ruthlessness but in fear and humility. All power is given to me in heaven and on earth: but it led him to lie naked and dead in the lap of his mother; for his work was to do the will of him that sent him, and all his life was a self-offering to his Father from whom alone the power came. We shall not use our powers aright unless we use them in the spirit of Christ washing his disciples' feet; we shall not use our powers aright unless like him we put them back into God's hands to be at his disposal. But if at all times we try to turn to God: to God our Father, in childlike trust and obedience; to God the Son our Friend, waiting to learn how we can fulfil friendship by sharing in his work and his sacrifice; to God the Spirit within us, listening for that inner voice which instructs the heart and begging him to identify our wills with us: then we can know that our power is in better hands than ours, in hands that will never abuse it as ours would because they are as gentle as they are strong.

There is something more. Respha sat guarding the bodies of her sons, *and suffered neither the birds to tear them by day nor the beasts by night.* Mary held her child in her arms in death as she had done in babyhood, the two moments of powerlessness. There is one use of power which is particularly divine and therefore particularly lovely: the use of power to protect or succour the powerless. To use the strength of your body to help those who are weak; to use the powers of your mind to help those who are less gifted; to use what material power or authority you may have to protect others; above all, to use the powers of your heart to bring comfort and strength and hope to those in sorrow and pain and distress: all this is power expressing love in deed. Always in the world there are men and women and children being torn by the evil birds of slander and scandalmongering and pharisaism, the wild beasts of cruelty, tyranny, hatred. Always the poor and weak and defenceless are at the mercy of man's injustice and rapacity; the gentle are at the mercy of the ruthless, the

72

humble at the mercy of the proud. When you support and defend them you share with Mary in the sublimity of her vocation—and you share with her in her devotion to her son, for inasmuch as these things are done to the least of his little ones they are done to him.

But you must first take haircloth, like Respha, the haircloth of penitence and humility; you must first be stripped and poor and naked; or you will do these things for your own sake rather than for the glory of God. The proud philanthropist can be one of humanity's worst enemies; he will use his gold for what seem to him to be good purposes, but being proud he will have no understanding of men's hearts and men's needs, no real sympathy for their sufferings; his charity will have something in it of the inhumanity of a bureaucratic regimentation of benefits. If ever your help has about it an atmosphere of condescension or impatience it will not be following the divine pattern: you can only help as God helps if, like him, you go down on your knees, knowing that this is not so much something you give as something you are given. Only to him who has nothing will much be given, that he may give to others. Only the poor in spirit can truly feed the hungry; only the naked can clothe the naked; only those who having nothing possess all things are given the power and the resources to harbour the harbourless, to lead home the homeless and the outcast and the lost.

The Seventh Sword

And he rolled a great stone to the door of the
sepulchre, and went his way.   MT. XXVII, 60

AND WENT HIS WAY: they are the words which close
the Stations of the Cross; and there is a terrible sort of
finality about them, like the clanging of a door upon
an empty world; you think of the church on Good
Friday when the Presence has gone from it and it is
now only a house, not a home. Yet that very emptiness,
since in fact it is very far from final, only serves to
underline for us the things we have been considering.
We have been thinking of freedom: freedom from fear,
from the tyranny of material things, from possessiveness, from self-pity, from depression, from the abuse of
power, from all the various forms of egoism; we have
been thinking of the one essential key to all these forms
of freedom, the sharing in Christ's death—stripped and
poor and naked—that leads to the sharing in his life
and his love. "You know well enough that we who
were taken up into Christ by baptism have been taken
up, all of us, into his death. In our baptism we have

77

been buried with him, died like him, that so, just as Christ was raised up by his Father's power from the dead, we too might live and move in a new kind of existence." [1]

In baptism we are buried in Christ, we begin to live a new kind of existence, because it reverses the order of sin, of egoism: it restores that order whereby God is at the centre of our lives, not our own ego; and so we are re-established in the *ordo universi*, the total pattern of creation; for the self-centred man is isolated, separate, cut off from his roots in this and in other worlds; but the God-centred man is planted again in the universe, living again in rhythm with the sun and the stars and earth, living again in harmony with the song of the spheres, because he is planted in the God of the universe.

But baptism is not an end but a beginning: it gives us the power to achieve, not the achievement. And we may fail. *He rolled a great stone to the door of the sepulchre and went his way*. It is so easy to lose vision and love. God gives you an insight into reality, a glimpse of himself, which would take you deep into his love and far in his service; but the superficialities call to you, the world unlit by vision calls to you, and you may roll a great stone between you and what you saw, and go your way, and the vision is lost. But *he* rolled the stone: it must always be ourselves, it is never God, who will erect the barrier: the only obstacles are those we make ourselves. God is always pursuing us with his love; it is we who try to escape, to blot out the vision. We blot it out by prolonged, deliberate disobedience; we blot it out by open rebellion, by hatred, to which pro-

[1] Romans VI, 4-5.

longed disobedience can lead; we blot it out by becoming hardened in indifference, which means indeed a gradual closing of all avenues to the greater world of eternity, a severing of all our roots, a stifling of all the deepest elements in our being, so that in the end, unless we turn back again, desolation inescapably follows, the immovable separateness and loneliness of hell.

But he rolled a *great* stone: God is not lightly lost to us; God is never lost to us so long as we go on trying, however unsuccessfully, to serve him. The little imperfections, the transitory semi-deliberate failings, the frailties: these can never be a great stone of separation. No sinfulness, however great, which leaves humility and love in the soul can ever be a great stone of separation. But good people imagine that God is lost to them because he feels remote from them; they blame themselves for loss of vision because it is dark night in their souls, but the dark night comes to them from God. The sinner is not an outcast from Christendom: he is at the very heart of Christendom, so long as there remains in him the will to turn to God, to go on searching for God and trying to serve him.

And just as the loss of stability and comfort, of friends and family, even to utter dereliction, may be sent us that we may learn to love God and find life; so too the loss of a sense of his presence, his inner reassurances and the joys of his service, may be sent us to ensure that we love him and not his gifts, to ensure that we are indeed stripped and poor and naked and are not pretending to ourselves that we love him when in reality we love only ourselves.

In the beginning the earth was void and empty, and darkness was upon the face of the deep; and the Spirit

79

of God moved over the waters. The tomb, the womb, the waters of chaos, these are the symbols for that nothingness, that self-annihilation of humility, out of which alone goodness and beauty can be created. We are to be buried with Christ that we may live and move in a new kind of existence: we are to be stripped of all life, all resources, all forms, that are self-ful, so that the Spirit may move over the waters of our chaos and re-create us, life springing anew from the womb, life springing anew from the tomb, the life of the new self which is the true self, identified with the self of Christ.

Then, as we saw before, we can hope to imitate Mary, not only in her motherhood, but in her enduring girlhood, her enduring strangeness to evil, even though our story hitherto has been a story of squalor. For indeed Christianity is precisely the religion which redeems humanity's squalors. When we lay ourselves bare to God's touch it can never be to a mere negation, a formlessness, that we strip ourselves: we are never pure negation, like the primeval chaos; we are privation, the waters dark and turbulent with ugliness and evil. But God was made sin for our sakes: it is into the depths of this squalor that the Word came; it is into the depths of this squalor that the Spirit comes to each individual soul, provided only that the sin can be transformed by creative sorrow. He rolled a great stone to the door of the sepulchre; and yet, great though it was, *valde mane sabbatorum*, very early in the morning, on the first day of the week, they found the stone rolled back. *Valde mane:* the night seems so long and so relentless, the darkness so black and impenetrable, but swiftly in the end the light comes. *Valde mane:* you would say the evil was irredeemable, the pride too entrenched, the sloth

80

too deeply embedded, the greed too tyrannical; but swiftly in the end the freedom comes. Depart from me, for I am a sinful man, O Lord: and in the very saying of the words the sin loses its stranglehold. O Lord, be merciful to me a sinner; and in the saying of the words the Temple is illumined, the mercy given. *Valde mane:* and in a moment the rose-red shaft of dawn strikes the open door of the tomb; and there in the garden is the Presence, radiant of eternity; and soon his mother will hear, will meet him, and no longer remember the anguish, for joy that her Son is reborn into the world, and that all humanity with him is reborn to a new heaven and a new earth.

Joy is the keynote of Christianity, just as surely as squalor is its raw material. The joy of the martyrs facing death for love; the joy of the saints who make themselves poor and outcast for love; the joy of the angels over one sinner repenting, the joy for the lost sheep, the joy for the lost groat; the joy of the sacraments, the joy of the Mass; all these are part of the one great paean of praise which is creation's purpose; and it is a song that is sung, not in forgetfulness of the squalor, not in defiance of the squalor, but as itself the transformation of the squalor. The spirit of God moved over the waters; and light was made; and God saw the light that it was good.

But the light and the song are not to remain merely creaturely, remote from the life of God. Through redeemed and love-possessed humanity they are taken up in Christ to the very heart of the Godhead, to join in that divine life which these sorrows of the Son have thrown open to us, the Trinity's own praise of the Godhead: the light growing more intense, more brilliant, more dazzling till it merges into the splendour of the light inaccessible; the song swelling and deepening till it merges into the harmony of the Uncreated Love.

And at the centre of that splendour and radiance and happiness there sits the Queen of the Seven Swords; and her song is still the song with which her life of motherhood began, and is the song too of all those children whom her motherhood has helped to save:

My soul doth magnify the Lord;
and my spirit hath rejoiced in God my Saviour;
Because he hath regarded the humility of his handmaid;
for behold from henceforth all generations shall call
me blessed;
For he that is mighty hath done great things to me and
holy is his name.